CHERYL T.LONG

Facing the fear of being alone

A journey through Emotional Isolation Book 1 in the Healing Through Wholeness Series

To every beautiful soul who has ever felt the weight of an empty evening or wondered if they're the only one who struggles with their own company.

To my younger self, who spent years believing she wasn't enough on her own.

And to you, dear reader, who dared to pick up this book. Your willingness to face what scares you gives everyone around you permission to heal as well.

This is for all of us learning that the thing we fear most might actually set us free.

"You are never alone when you

are with yourself."

— Unknown

Contents

Preface

Hey Friend, Let's Talk

Listen, can we be real for a minute?

I'm not writing this book because I'm some kind of expert who has it all figured out. I'm writing it because I've been exactly where you are right now - terrified of being alone, making decisions based on that fear, and feeling like maybe I was the only person on the planet who couldn't handle my own company.

Spoiler alert: I wasn't the only one, and neither are you. This book? It's me sitting across from you with a cup of coffee,

sharing what I've learned, what's worked, what hasn't, and what I wish someone had told me years ago when I was scrolling through my phone at 11 PM, hoping *someone* would text me back so I wouldn't have to face another quiet evening.

Here's What We're Going to Do Together

I'm going to walk with you through this. Not ahead of you like some guru, but right beside you like the friend who gets it because she's been there too.

We're going to start small - like, really small. Because I know how overwhelming it can feel when someone tells you to "just enjoy being alone!" when the thought of it makes your chest tight.

We're going to figure out:

- What's going on when you feel that panic about being alone
- Where this stuff comes from (it's not your fault, by the way)
- Some simple things you can try that won't make you feel worse
- How to be gentle with yourself through this process
- How to Build Up Your Confidence for the Bigger Changes Ahead. And here's the thing - this is just the beginning. I've got a whole other book ("You're Not Alone") that goes way deeper into all of this, with workbook exercises and everything. But you need this foundation first. Please think of this book as us becoming friends, and the next one as us rolling up our sleeves and doing the real work together.

One More Thing

I want you to know that picking up this book is already a brave act. I know it might not feel brave - it might feel desperate or embarrassing or scary. But choosing to face something that terrifies you? That's courage, even if your hands are shaking while you do it.

Preface

You're already doing the work just by being here. Are you ready to figure this out together?

Love, Cheryl

Introduction

******

The Journey Begins

Dear friend,

If you've picked up this book, I want you to know something right away: **you are not broken**.

The fear of being alone, whether it's for an evening, a weekend, or the more profound fear of being truly on your own in life, is one of the most human experiences there is. Yet so many of us suffer in silence, believing we're the only ones who feel this way.

I know because I've been there.

My Story

For most of my life, I was never truly alone. I went from one relationship straight into the next throughout my teens, and even through my marriages. I couldn't handle the thought of being by myself.

When I had my children, I made sure our house was always packed, not just with my kids, but with their friends, neighbors, anyone who would fill the space and the silence. I was the mom who encouraged sleepovers and playdates, not just because

I loved having kids around (though I did), but because the alternative—a quiet house—felt unbearable.

I told myself I was just being social, just being a good mom. But the truth was, I was terrified of being alone with myself. I didn't even know who I was when no one else was around.

This pattern followed me through three marriages. I stayed in relationships that had run their course, not because I was happy, but because single meant alone, and alone felt like drowning.

Then life forced my hand. My third husband and I separated, and shortly after, he passed away. For the first time in my adult life, really, for the first time since I was a teenager, I was truly on my own.

Yes, I had a male friend who provided some support, but this was different. This was the first time I had to depend solely on myself. Pay my bills, make my own decisions, sit with my thoughts, face my fears, all of it, by myself.

I won't lie to you, it was terrifying at first. There were nights when the silence felt so heavy I could barely breathe. There were moments when I almost called someone, anyone, to hear another voice. But something incredible happened in that space. Slowly, gradually, I started to discover who I was when no one else was around. I learned that I could handle my own company.

I realized that being alone and being lonely weren't the same thing. I knew that some of my most peaceful, creative, and healing moments happened when it was just me.

Why This Book Exists

This book exists because transformation is possible. Not just coping, not just managing, but genuine transformation where solitude becomes a source of strength rather than fear.

This isn't about becoming a hermit or never needing people again. It's about building such a strong, loving relationship with yourself that you can choose connection from a place of fullness rather than desperate need.

What You'll Discover

In this book, you'll learn:

You're not alone in feeling alone - Millions of people struggle with this fear

Where these fears come from - Understanding the root makes change possible

Simple, practical steps you can take starting today - No overwhelming transformations, just gentle progress

How to build a support system for this journey - Because healing happens in community, too

That there's so much more available to you - This fear

has been limiting your life in ways you might not even realize

A Gentle Beginning

This book is designed to be a gentle beginning. We're not diving into the deepest waters right away. Instead, we're starting at the shore, letting you get comfortable with the idea that the water isn't as scary as it seemed from a distance.

Think of this as your foundation book—the place where you build the solid ground from which all other growth becomes possible. Book 2 in this series, "You're Not Alone," will take you much deeper, offering comprehensive tools for complete transformation. But that deeper work is only possible when you have this foundation in place.

You're Already Brave

The fact that you're reading this book means you're already braver than you might realize. It means you're ready to face what has felt too scary to face. It means you're choosing growth over comfort, truth over familiar pain.

That's the definition of courage: not the absence of fear, but moving forward despite it.

How to Use Your Fear

Here's something that might surprise you: your fear isn't your enemy. It's been trying to protect you, even if it's been doing so in ways that have limited your life. Throughout this book, we'll learn to work *with* your fear rather than against it.

You'll discover that the fear of being alone often masks a more profound wisdom, a knowing that you deserve more than you've been accepting, that you're meant for deeper connections and more authentic living.

What's Possible

As we journey through these pages together, I want you to start imagining what might be possible:

Evenings at home that feel peaceful rather than empty

The ability to make decisions based on what you truly want, not what will keep you from being alone

Relationships chosen from love rather than fear

A deep, unshakeable sense of your worth and completeness

The freedom to say no when you need space and yes when you genuinely want connection

A life that feels authentically yours

These aren't just dreams—they're possibilities that become realities when you do this work.

We're in This Together

As you read these words, know that you're not taking this journey alone. I'm here with you, and so are the thousands of others who have walked this path before you and the thousands who will walk it after.

Your willingness to face your fear doesn't just heal you; it permits everyone around you to do the same. Your courage creates ripples that touch lives you'll never even know about.

Ready to Begin?

In the pages that follow, we'll start gently. We'll begin by simply recognizing and understanding your fear, not trying to fix it or make it go away, but getting to know it like you would a new neighbor.

Then, step by step, page by page, we'll build your capacity to be with yourself in ways that feel nourishing rather than frightening.

By the end of this book, you won't be "cured" of ever feeling afraid of being alone; that's not the goal. But you will have built a foundation of understanding, self-compassion, and practical tools that will support you for the rest of your life.

And you'll be ready for the more profound transformation that awaits in Book 2.

Take a deep breath. You're exactly where you're supposed to be.

With love and solidarity,

Cheryl

Part One

Chapter 1

Let's Name What's Happening

Okay, so picture this: It's Sunday afternoon, and your friend just texted to cancel your dinner plans. Your first thought isn't "Oh well, I'll make something nice

for myself." It's more like "Oh God, now what am I going to do with my entire evening?"

Sound familiar?

Or maybe you're the person who keeps the TV on from the moment you walk in the door until you fall asleep, not because you're watching anything, but because the silence feels too heavy.

Or you find yourself saying yes to hanging out with people you don't even really enjoy, just because the alternative - being home alone - feels worse.

Listen, I see you. I've been you.

What Are We Dealing With Her?

The fancy term is "monophobia" - fear of being alone. But

I hate when we put clinical labels on very human experiences, because it makes it sound like you have some rare condition instead of an understandable response to being human.

Here's what's happening: You've learned somewhere along the way that being alone isn't safe. Not physically unsafe (usually), but emotionally unsafe. Like being alone means something bad about you, or something bad will happen, or you won't be able to handle whatever comes up when it's just you and your thoughts.

How This Shows Up in Real Lif*e*

Let me guess - you might recognize some of these:

The Panic Scramble: It's Friday at 5 PM, and you realize you have no plans. Cue the frantic texting: "Anyone want to grab dinner?" "Movie night at someone's house?" Anything to avoid a quiet evening.

The Yes Woman/Man: You say yes to everything, even when you're exhausted, even when you don't want to go, because saying no means being alone.

The Background Noise: Your apartment is never quiet. TV, music, podcasts - anything to fill the space so you don't have to hear your thoughts.

The Relationship Cling: You stay in relationships way past their expiration date, not because you're happy, but because being single feels terrifying, and alone feels even more so.

The Activity Addict: Your calendar is packed. Gym, work events, volunteering, social plans - if there's a free moment, you fill it.

What It Feels Like Inside

When you think about being alone - really alone, with nothing to distract you - what happens in your body?

For me, it used to feel like this weight on my chest, like I couldn't quite catch my breath. My mind would start racing: "What if I get sad and can't shake it? What if I start thinking about everything that's wrong with my life? What if I realize how lonely I am?"

Maybe for you it's different. Maybe it's restlessness, like you literally can't sit still. Or perhaps it's this empty feeling, like something essential is missing.

Whatever it is, it's real, and it makes perfect sense.

The Story Your Mind Tells You

Here's what I've learned: the fear of being alone is rarely actually about being alone. It's about what being alone means in the story we tell ourselves.

Familiar stories I hear (and lived myself):

- "If I'm alone, it means no one wants to be with me."
- "If I'm alone, I'll fall apart and won't be able to put myself back together."
- "If I'm alone, I'll have to face things I'm not ready to face."

- "If I'm alone, it proves I'm not interesting/lovable/worthy enough."

What story does your mind tell you about what being alone means?

The Hidden Costs of Avoiding Alone Time

Living in fear of solitude costs us more than we realize:

Decision Fatigue: When every choice is filtered through "will this keep me from being alone?" you exhaust yourself making decisions that aren't really about what you want.

Lost Authenticity: You might not even know what you enjoy anymore because you've been so focused on what keeps you connected to others.

Relationship Pressure: Other people can feel overwhelmed by your need for constant connection, which can push them away.

Missed Opportunities: How many experiences have you said no to because they required being alone?

Financial Drain: Constantly eating out, going to movies, and buying things to avoid being home adds up.

But Here's the Thing…

None of this makes you weak or broken or pathetic. It makes you human.

We're wired for connection. For most of human history, being alone actually could be dangerous. Your nervous system is doing what it evolved to do - keep you safe by keeping you connected.

The problem is that in our modern world, being alone isn't usually dangerous. It's often precisely what we need to figure out who we are and what we want.

The First Step: Just Noticing

Right now, I don't want you to try to change anything. I want you to start noticing.

This week, when you feel that familiar anxiety about being alone, pause and think: "Oh, there it is. That's my fear of being alone showing up."

No judgment. No, trying to fix it. Just recognition.

Like if you had a friend who always knocked on your door at the same time every day. You wouldn't be surprised or angry - you'd think, "Oh, there's my friend again." Can you start to relate to your fear in that way? Not as an enemy, but as something familiar that shows up predictably?

Why Recognition Matters

When you can recognize what's happening, you're no longer being controlled by it unconsciously. You move from "I have to do something RIGHT NOW, not to be alone" to "Oh, I'm feeling afraid of being alone right now."

That pause, that moment of recognition, is where your power lives.

What's Coming Next

In the next chapter, we're going to explore where this fear might have come from. Not to blame anyone or make excuses, but because understanding the "why" makes the "how to change" so much clearer.

For now, practice noticing. You're already doing something brave by being willing to look at this stuff.

I'm proud of you for starting.

Your Turn: Let's Get Real

Grab a journal, your phone notes, or just a piece of paper. I want you to be honest about your own experience. Remember, no one else has to see this.

When does your fear of being alone show up most?

- Sunday evenings?
- When do plans get canceled?
- When you're going through a hard time?
- When you're happy and worry, it won't last?

What does it feel like in your body?

- Racing heart?
- Tight chest?
- Restless legs?
- Stomach knots?

What story does your mind tell you about being alone?

Complete this sentence: "If I'm alone, it means…"

How has this fear been trying to protect you? Fears usually develop for good reasons. How might your fear of being alone have been trying to take care of you?

What has avoiding being alone cost you?

- Energy?
- Money?
- Authentic relationships?
- Opportunities?
- Self-knowledge?

Take your time with this. And remember, awareness without judgment is the ultimate goal.

Ready for Chapter 2? Let's figure out where this all started...

Chapter 2

Where Did This Fear Come From? (And Why It's Not Your Fault)

Alright, so now that we've named what's happening, you're probably wondering: "But WHY do I feel this way? What's wrong with me that I can't just be okay

alone like other people seem to be?"

First off, nothing is wrong with you. Let me say that again louder for the people in the back: **NOTHING IS WRONG WITH YOU.**

Second, other people aren't as okay with being alone as they might appear. Trust me on this one.

But let's talk about where this fear might have started, because understanding the "why" can be such a relief. It's like finally having an explanation for something that's been confusing you for years.

It Started Way Before You Realized

Here's something that might blow your mind: you learned whether being alone was safe or scary before you could even talk.

I'm not trying to get all psychology-heavy on you, but stick with me here because this is important.

When you were a baby, your survival depended on the care and support of others. If you were left alone, you could die. So your little nervous system developed this alarm system that went off whenever the people you needed weren't there.

For some of us, that alarm system never really learned to calm down.

Family Patterns (No Blame, Just Understanding)

Think back to your childhood home. What was the vibe around being alone?

Maybe you had parents who couldn't stand quiet moments either - always had the TV on, always busy, always going somewhere. You learned that silence and solitude weren't comfortable.

Or maybe you had parents who were so anxious about you being alone that they transmitted that fear to you. "Don't go in your room by yourself, come sit with the family." "What are you doing up there all alone?" The message: alone = something's wrong.

Or the flip side - maybe your parents were never around, and being alone meant you'd been forgotten or weren't important enough for their time.

Maybe being alone was when bad things happened - when parents fought, when scary thoughts crept in, when you felt the weight of family problems that were too big for a kid to carry. **Here's what I want you to know**: Whatever happened in your childhood, your parents were probably doing their best with what they knew. This isn't about blame. It's about understanding why your nervous system might have learned that alone = danger.

Cultural Messages (They're Everywhere)

Our whole culture is messed up about being alone, honestly. Think about it:

- Every Disney movie ends with the princess finding her prince.
- Being single is often viewed as a problem to be solved.
- "Alone" gets used as a synonym for "lonely" or "sad."
- We ask people, "Are you here by yourself?" as if it's something to be pitied.

From the time we're tiny, we get messages that being coupled up, busy, and socially active is the goal. Being alone is portrayed as either scary (horror movies love an isolated victim) or depressing (the cat lady stereotype).

No wonder so many of us feel like something's wrong when we're by ourselves.

Past Experiences that Stuck

Sometimes the fear of being alone gets locked in by specific experiences.

Maybe you were left alone when you were too young and got scared.

Maybe you were alone when you got terrible news.

Maybe the first time you lived by yourself, something fright- ening happened.

Maybe you were alone during a panic attack, and now your brain links the two together.

Being alone can lead to overthinking and spiraling into dark places.

Our brains are good at making connections: "This bad thing happened when I was alone, so being alone = bad things happen."

The Modern Isolation Paradox

Here's something weird about our current world: we're more connected than ever through technology, but we're also more isolated than previous generations.

We can text someone any time of day, scroll through social media to see what everyone's doing, and binge-watch shows to feel like we have company. However, all that artificial connection can make genuine solitude feel more frightening by comparison.

Additionally, we've lost some of the natural community that once existed. Extended families living together, neighbors who knew each other, churches, or community centers where people gathered regularly. Many of us are much more on our own than humans have ever been in history.

So, when you feel scared of being alone, part of what you might be feeling is the bigger cultural loneliness that many of us are experiencing.

Your Nervous System is Just Doing Its Job

Here's what I want you to understand: if you struggle with being alone, your nervous system isn't broken. It's working exactly as it's supposed to, based on what it learned.

If being alone. Due to real danger or just a perceived sense of danger, your nervous system stores that information as if you had ever felt unsafe at some point. Now it's just trying to keep you safe the way it knows how.

The problem is that what once protected you might now be limiting you.

It's like having a dedicated security guard who learned that anyone wearing red is dangerous. Even years later, when the red-wearing threat is long gone, that security guard is still sounding the alarm every time someone in red walks by. The security guard isn't wrong or broken - they're just working with outdated information.

The Good News

Understanding where your fear came from is incredibly freeing because it helps you realize:

1. **It made sense**: Your fear developed for good

reasons.

2. **It's not personal**: This isn't about you being weak or flawed.
3. **It can change**: What was learned can be unlearned.
4. **You're not alone**: Millions of people have similar stories

It's Not About Finding Someone to Blame

I want to be clear about something: figuring out where your fear came from isn't about finding someone to blame or dwelling on past hurts.

It's about understanding so you can have compassion for yourself and make informed choices about what you want to do differently in the future.

Your parents, your ex-partners, your past experiences - they all did what they did. You can't change that. But you can change how you respond to your fear now.

What This Means for Your Healing

Knowing that your fear has roots - that it didn't just appear out of nowhere - can be comforting. It means:

- You're not crazy
- You're not weak
- You're not broken
- You're just human, responding in very human ways to very human experiences

And it means that healing is possible, because what was

learned can be unlearned. What was conditioned can be reconditioned. Neural pathways that were formed can be reformed.

Moving Forward with Self-Compassion

As we move into the next chapter, where we'll start taking some small steps toward change, I want you to carry this understanding with you:

Your fear of being alone is not your fault. It was developed for good reasons, and it's been trying to protect you. You can acknowledge it, thank it for trying to keep you safe, and then gently start teaching it that you're safe now, even when you're alone.

You're not trying to eliminate this fear—that's not realistic or necessary. You're just trying to have a different relationship with it, one where it doesn't run your life.

Ready to start taking some baby steps together?

Let's Get Curious About Your Story

I want you to explore your own origin story, but gently. If anything feels too heavy or evokes difficult emotions, please be gentle with yourself. You can always come back to this later or discuss it with a counselor.

Childhood Patterns:

- What was the vibe in your house around being alone?
- How did your family handle quiet time or

solitude?

- What messages did you get about being by yourself?

Early Experiences:

- Can you remember the first time you felt scared to be alone?
- Were there any specific incidents that made you feel unsafe when alone?
- What was happening in your life during times when the fear felt strongest?

Cultural/Social Messages:

- What did the adults around you teach you about relation- ships and being single?
- How did your friend groups handle alone time?
- What messages from movies, books, or media stick with you about being alone?

Your Nervous System:

- When you think about being alone, what's the first feeling that comes up?
- Where do you feel that emotion in your body?
- If your fear could talk, what would it say it's trying to protect you from?

Remember: This is about understanding, not judgment. You're getting to know your fear like you'd get to know a new friend - with curiosity and compassion.

Chapter 3

Taking the First Tiny Steps (Seriously, They're Tiny)

Now that you understand what you're dealing with and have some idea of its origin, you can proceed with confidence. You might be feeling like, "Great, now what? How do I fix this?"

Here's the thing - we're not trying to "fix" anything. We're just going to start getting a little more comfortable with the idea that you can handle being with yourself.

And we're going to start stupidly small. Like, embarrassingly small. Because that's how real change happens.

Why We Start Small (Really Small)

I know you might be thinking, "Just tell me how to love being alone! Give me the big solution!" But here's what I've learned: when you're scared of something, the worst thing you can do is force yourself into the deep end.

If you're afraid of water, I'm not going to throw you in the ocean. We're going to start by getting your toes wet in the kiddie pool.

Starting small means:

- Your nervous system doesn't freak out.
- You can succeed (which builds confidence)
- You prove to yourself that you CAN handle this.
- You don't overwhelm yourself and give up

The Magic of Micro-Moments

We're going to work with what I call "micro-moments" - tiny periods of intentional alone time that feel manageable.

Think 5 minutes, not 5 hours. Think of sitting in your car before going inside, not spending a weekend by yourself. Think of turning off the TV during a commercial, not having a silent retreat.

These micro-moments are like little experiments: "Can I handle being alone with my thoughts for just this tiny bit of time?"

Most of the time, you'll discover you can. And each time you can, you're building evidence that being alone isn't dangerous.

Your First Micro-Moment: The Five-Minute Sit

Here's your first tiny experiment, and I mean TINY:

Today, sit alone for five minutes with no distractions.

That's it. No phone, no TV, no music, no book. Just you, sitting somewhere comfortable, for five whole minutes.

Set a timer so you're not wondering how much time is left.

What might happen:

- Your mind might race.
- You might feel restless.
- You might notice anxiety in your body.
- You might feel bored.
- You might feel... fine?

What to do with whatever happens:

- Please take a look at it without judging it.
- Remind yourself: "This is just five minutes, I can handle five minutes."
- If anxiety comes up, breathe slowly and remind yourself you're safe.
- If your mind races, that's normal - you don't have to stop the thoughts, don't follow them down rabbit holes

After the five minutes:

- Could you give yourself credit for doing it?
- Notice: Did you survive? (Spoiler alert: you did)
- Write down what you noticed - not to analyze it, to remember

Building Your Comfort Zone Gradually

Once you can do five minutes without significant distress, try ten minutes. Then fifteen. There's no rush - this could take weeks or months, and that's perfectly fine.

The goal isn't to become someone who loves hours of solitude (though that might happen eventually). The goal is to prove to yourself that you can handle being alone for reasonable periods without feeling overwhelmed or falling apart.

The Car Experiment

Here's another tiny step that's surprisingly powerful:

When you get home, sit in your car for five minutes before going inside.

This works because:

- You're not technically "alone" - you're just transitioning.
- It's time-limited (you're going inside soon)
- It's a bridge between being out in the world and being home alone.
- You get to practice the feeling without the full commitment Use this time to:
    - Take some deep breaths.
    - Please take a moment to assess how your body feels.
    - Could you set an intention for your evening?
    - Appreciate that you're giving yourself this small gift

The Commercial Break Practice

If five minutes of complete silence feels too intense, try this:

During TV commercial breaks, refrain from checking your phone or doing anything else. Just sit with the silence. Most commercials are 2-3 minutes long, so it's even shorter than our five-minute practice. But you're training yourself to be okay with moments of quiet and unstimulated time.

Dealing with the Uncomfortable Feelings

When you try these tiny experiments, uncomfortable feelings will probably come up. That's not a sign that you're doing it wrong - it's a sign that you're doing it right.

If anxiety shows up:

- Remind yourself that feelings are temporary.
- Breathe slowly and deeply.
- Tell yourself: "This feeling is uncomfortable, but I'm not in danger."
- Remember that anxiety often peaks and then naturally decreases

If sadness comes up:

- Could you please leave it as is without trying to fix it?
- Sometimes being still allows emotions we've been avoiding to surface

- This isn't bad - it's healthy.
- The sadness was probably already there; you're just noticing it now

If boredom hits:

- Welcome to being human! Boredom is normal
- You don't have to entertain yourself every second.
- Boredom often leads to creativity or interesting thoughts if you let it.
- Think of it as your mind taking a rest

If your mind races:

- This is super common.
- You don't have to stop your thoughts.
- Try thinking of them like background noise - acknowledge them, but don't engage.
- Some people find it helpful to mentally say "thinking" when they notice their mind spinning.

The Self-Compassion Part (This is Crucial)

Here's what I need you to remember as you try these tiny steps: **be ridiculously kind to yourself.**

If you try the five-minute sit and last only two minutes before you grab your phone, you didn't fail. You lasted two minutes longer than you have before!

If you feel anxious, sad, or restless, you're not doing it wrong. You're just being human.

This isn't about becoming a meditation master or someone who never feels uncomfortable alone. It's about building up your tolerance gradually, like strengthening a muscle.

What Success Looks Like

Success isn't:

- Never feeling anxious when alone.
- Immediately loving solitude
- Being able to meditate for hours
- Never wanting company Success IS:
- Trying the experiment, even if it's hard
- Lasting a little longer each time
- Noticing your feelings without being overwhelmed by them
- Being kind to yourself through the process
- Building evidence that you can handle being with yourself

Keep Track of Your Wins

I want you to celebrate every tiny victory, because they add up to significant changes.

Keep a simple log:

- "Tried five-minute sit - felt restless but did it"
- "Sat in car for three minutes - noticed I was okay"
- "Made it through two commercial breaks without checking phone."

These might seem insignificant, but they're not. Each time you choose to be present with yourself instead of immediately seeking distraction, you're rewiring your brain's understanding of what's safe.

What's Next

Once you've become comfortable with these micro-moments (and I mean relaxed, not thrilled, just not panicked), we'll start expanding them and adding new elements.

For now, I'd like you to focus on these small steps. They're the foundation everything else builds on.

Remember: You're not trying to become a different person. You're just getting to know the person you already are.

Your Tiny Step Action Plan

Could you pick ONE of these to try this week? Just one. We're going stupidly slow on purpose.

Option 1: The Five-Minute Sit

- Could you set a timer for 5 minutes?
- Sit somewhere comfortable
- No phone, TV, music, or distractions
- Just breathe and notice what happens.
- Do this once a day for a week

Option 2: The Car Pause

- When you get home, stay in your car for 5

minutes.
- Turn off the radio/music.
- Just sit and breathe before going inside.
- Notice what you're feeling without trying to change it

Option 3: Commercial Break Practice

- During TV commercial breaks, could you put down your phone?
- Don't get up to do tasks.
- Just sit with the quiet for those 2-3 minutes.
- Do this for all commercials during one show

Track Your Experience: Each day, write down:

- Which exercise did you try?
- How long did you last
- What did you notice in your body?
- What thoughts came up
- How did you feel afterward?
- One thing to appreciate about yourself for trying

Remember: There's no perfect way to do this. There's only your way, and your way is exactly right.

Chapter 4

Building Your Foundation (The Practical Stuff)

Alright, so you've been practicing your tiny moments of alone time. Maybe it's feeling a little easier, or perhaps it still feels hard, but you're doing it anyway. Either

way, I'm proud of you.

Now, we're going to discuss setting yourself up for success. Because here's the thing - if your environment makes being alone feel terrible, you're fighting an uphill battle.

Making Your Space Feel Safe

Let's be honest: if your home feels chaotic, lonely, or depress- ing, of course, you don't want to be there alone.

But here's the good news - you can change that, and you don't need a big budget or interior design skills.

Start with the basics:

- Is your space clean enough to feel peaceful rather than stressful?

- Do you have at least one spot where you feel comfortable sitting quietly?
- Is there natural light during the day?
- Can you control the temperature so you're physically comfortable?

I'm not talking about Pinterest-perfect here. I'm talking about "this feels like a place where I can relax", basic.

Create one "safe" spot: Pick one corner, one chair, one spot in your home that's going to be your go-to place for alone time. Make it as comfortable as possible:

- A soft blanket you love
- Good lighting (lamp, not harsh overhead)
- Maybe a plant or something beautiful to look at
- Keep it clutter-free
- This is your spot for when you want to practice being with yourself

The Sound Situation

Here's something I learned the hard way: you don't have to go from constant noise to complete silence overnight.

Option 1: Gradual Quiet

- Start by turning down the volume on whatever you usually have on
- Try softer background sounds, such as rain, gentle instru- mental music, or nature sounds.
- Gradually decrease the volume over time.

- Eventually, try short periods of complete quiet.

Option 2: Comfortable Sounds. Maybe silence isn't your goal right now, and that's okay. Some people find these sounds comforting during alone time:

- Soft instrumental music
- Nature sounds (rain, ocean, forest)
- Coffee shop ambiance
- Very quiet, familiar TV shows (like reruns where you know what happens)

The goal is to feel comfortable, not to meet some standard of what solitude "should" look like.

Timing Matters

When you practice being alone, it matters more than you might think.

Best times to start:

- When you're already naturally calm (not stressed or anx- ious)
- When you have energy (not when you're exhausted and vulnerable)
- During daylight hours (darkness can make everything feel more intense)
- On days when you don't have big, stressful things happen- ing

Times to maybe avoid while you're building this skill:

- Late at night, when everything feels more dramatic

- When you're already emotional about something else
- Right after consuming news or social media
- When you're hungry, tired, or physically uncomfortable

The Phone Question

Let's talk about the elephant in the room: your phone.

I'm not going to tell you to throw it in a drawer and never look at it. However, I would suggest that having it within arm's reach makes it hard to sit with any uncomfortable feelings.

What works for many people:

- Put the phone in another room during your alone time practice.
- Or put it on airplane mode.
- Or at least turn it face down so you can't see notifications.
- Set specific times for checking it, rather than having it available constantly

The goal is to prove to yourself that you can handle whatever feelings come up without immediately reaching for distraction.

Having a Plan for Difficult Moments

Sometimes when you're alone, complex thoughts or feelings will surface. Having a plan ahead of time makes this less scary.

When anxiety shows up:

- Remind yourself that anxiety is temporary.
- Use slow, deep breathing.
- Name five things you can see, four you can hear, three you can touch.
- Remember that feeling anxious doesn't mean you're in danger

When sadness appears:

- Let it be there without trying to fix it immediately.
- Sometimes sadness wants to be acknowledged.
- Wrap yourself in a soft blanket.
- Remember that being sad doesn't mean you're broken

When loneliness hits:

- Distinguish between being alone and being lonely (they're not the same thing)
- Remember that you can feel lonely even when surrounded by people.
- Could you consider reaching out to someone after your alone time practice is done?
- Practice talking to yourself with kindness.

When scary thoughts come up:

- Remind yourself that thoughts are not facts.
- You don't have to believe or engage with every thought you have

- You can try to observe the thoughts without getting caught up in them.
- If thoughts feel overwhelming or concerning, reach out to a friend or counselor.

Building Gentle Routines

Structure can be comforting when you're learning to be alone.

A simple alone time routine might look like:

- Make a cup of tea or coffee.
- Please feel free to sit in your comfortable spot.
- Take five deep breaths.
- Could you set your timer for the duration of your practice?
- After the timer goes off, do something kind for yourself

Or:

- Light a candle
- Put on soft music
- Sit quietly and observe your space.
- When you're done, write down one thing you appreciated about the experience.

Having a routine makes it feel less scary and more intentional.

The Budd5 S5stem (Yes, Even for Leavening to Be Alone)

Here's something that might seem contradictory: having support from others can help you get more comfortable being alone.

Tell a trusted friend what you're working on:

- They can check in on how it's going.
- You can text them before and after your alone time practice.
- They can remind you of your progress when you feel discouraged.
- Just knowing someone is rooting for you makes it easier

Join online communities:

- There are forums and groups for people working on similar things.
- You can share experiences and get encouragement.
- Knowing you're not the only one helps normalize the experience

What to Do When It Feels Too Have

Some days, your alone time practice is going to feel difficult. That's normal.

On the hard days:

- Reduce the time (try 2 minutes instead of 5)
- Could you make the environment extra

comfortable?

- Remind yourself that hard days don't mean you're failing.
- Consider what else is going on in your life that might be making it more challenging.
- Be extra gentle with yourself.

If it consistently feels overwhelming:

- You might need to slow down even more.
- Could you consider whether there are deeper issues that need professional support?
- Remember that asking for help is a sign of bravery, not weakness.
- A counselor can help you work through underlying anxiety or trauma

<u>Building Your Confidence Gvaduall5</u>

Every time you sit alone for your planned amount of time - even if it feels uncomfortable you're building evidence that you can handle being with yourself.

Keep track of your wins:

- "Day 1: Felt restless but stayed for the full 5 minutes"
- "Day 3: Felt peaceful for a moment"
- "Day 7: Didn't feel like I needed to turn on TV after immediately"

Notice the changes:

- Are you lasting longer without checking your

phone?
- Do you feel slightly less anxious when alone?
- Are you beginning to enjoy any moments of it?
- Are you making decisions less based on avoiding alone time?

The Goal Isn't Perfect Peace

I want to manage your expectations here: the goal isn't to become someone who feels blissfully peaceful every moment you're alone.

The goal is to become someone who can be with whatever comes up - restlessness, sadness, anxiety, boredom - without immediately needing to escape from it.

Sometimes alone time will feel hard, and that's okay. Some- times it will feel neutral, and that's okay too. Sometimes it might feel good, and that's a bonus.

What's Coming Next

In our next chapter, we will discuss expanding these skills and taking on some tasks that might feel a little scarier, such as eating a meal alone or going for a walk.

But that's later. For now, focus on building this foundation: a comfortable space, manageable periods, and the knowledge that you can handle whatever feelings come up.

You're doing something courageous by learning to be with yourself. Not everyone is willing to do this work.

Your Foundation Checklist

Take your time with this. You don't need to do everything at once.

Creating Your Space:

- ☐ I have one spot in my home that feels peaceful
- ☐ This spot is comfortable and has good lighting
- ☐ I've removed or minimized clutter from this area
- ☐ I have a soft blanket or something comforting nearby
- ☐ I've made this space feel welcoming to me

Managing Sound:

- ☐ I've experimented with different sound levels
- ☐ I know what background noise (if any) feels comfortable
- ☐ I can create periods of quiet when I want them
- ☐ I'm not dependent on constant loud noise to feel okay

Phone/Technology:

- ☐ I can put my phone away during alone time practice
- ☐ I've found a way to minimize distractions
- ☐ I'm not checking my phone compulsively during quiet time

Timing:

- ☐ I've identified good times of day for my practice

☐ I avoid practicing when I'm already stressed or tired

☐ I've built some routine around my alone time

Support System:

☐ At least one person knows I'm working on this

☐ I have someone I can reach out to if I need encouragement

☐ I know when to seek professional help if needed

Coping Strategies:

☐ I have a plan for when anxiety comes up

☐ I know what to do if I feel sad during alone time

☐ I can distinguish between uncomfortable and unsafe

☐ I practice self-compassion when things feel hard

Progress Tracking:

☐ I'm keeping track of my small wins

☐ I notice improvements, even tiny ones

☐ I celebrate my courage in doing this work

Remember: You don't need to be perfect at any of this. You need to be willing to try.

Are you ready for Chapter 5? Let's talk about taking this into the real world...

Chapter 5

Small Acts of Courage (AKA: Doing Stuff by Yourself Without Dying)

Okay, so you've been practicing sitting alone in your safe space, and maybe it's starting to feel less like torture and more like... well, something you can handle.

Now comes the part that might make your palms a little sweaty: doing things on your own out in the world.

But before you panic and close this book, could you hear me out? We're still going tiny here. I'm not suggesting you take yourself on a solo vacation to Europe. I'm talking about baby steps that happen to involve leaving your house.

Why This Matters

Here's the thing about only practicing solitude at home: your brain might start to think, "Okay, I can handle being alone in my safe space, but that doesn't count for the real world."

When you start doing small activities alone in public, you prove to yourself that:

- You can enjoy your own company anywhere.
- Other people don't care as much as you think they do
- You're capable of handling whatever comes up.
- Being alone doesn't make you weird or pathetic.

Plus, some of my favorite memories now are things I did by myself. Things I would have missed if I'd waited for someone to go with me.

The "Everyone's Watching Me" Fear

Let's address this head-on because I know it's probably what you're thinking: "But what will people think if they see me alone?"

Here's what I've learned from years of doing stuff by myself: **most people are way too busy thinking about their own lives to judge you for being alone.**

And the ones who do notice? They're probably thinking one of these things:

- "Good for her, I wish I were confident enough to do that."
- "She looks peaceful."
- Nothing at all, because they glanced at you for 2 seconds and moved on

The judgment you're worried about is happening way more in your head than in reality.

Starting Stupid Small: The Coffee Shop Test

Here's your first tiny solo adventure: **Get a coffee or tea by yourself.**

I know, I know. "But Cheryl, I do that all the time!" you might be thinking. But I'm talking about something specific:

The Coffee Shop Sit:

- Go to a coffee shop
- Order your drink
- Sit down at a table (not takeout)
- Stay for at least 10 minutes.
- Don't immediately pull out your phone.
- Just sit with your drink and observe your surroundings

That's it. No reading, no working, no calling someone. Just you, your coffee, and the experience of being alone in public.

What might happen:

- You might feel self-conscious at first.
- You might want to grab your phone immediately.
- You might notice other people and wonder what they're thinking.
- You might start to relax after a few minutes.
- You might realize it's kind of nice

If it feels too intense:

- Start with just 5 minutes.
- You can pick a busy coffee shop where you can blend in more.
- Go during busy times when everyone's focused on their stuff.
- Bring a book as backup, but try to spend some time without it

The Solo Walk (*Nature Edition*)

If coffee shops feel too social, try this: **Take a 15-minute walk by yourself.**

The rules:

- No podcasts, music, or phone calls
- Just you, walking, noticing your surroundings.
- If you see other people, smile or nod if it feels natural.
- Pay attention to what you notice when you're not distracted

Why this works:

- Movement can help with anxiety.
- Nature (even city nature) is naturally calming.
- Walking gives you a physical activity to engage in.
- You're practicing being alone but not trapped anywhere

Pro tip: If your neighborhood doesn't feel safe for solo walks, try a local park during daylight hours when other people are around.

The Solo Meal *(Start Small)*

This is the one that terrifies most people: eating alone in public. So we're going to ease into it.

Level 1: The Lunch Counter

- Go to a casual place with counter seating (deli, café, diner)
- Sit at the counter (it feels less exposed than a table)
- Order something simple
- Eat your meal without your phone for at least half of it.
- Notice the experience without judging it.

Why counter seating works:

- You're facing away from most people.
- It feels more natural to eat alone at a counter.
- There's usually stuff to look at (kitchen, other people ordering)
- It's temporary (you eat and leave)

Level 2: The Table for One. Once counter eating feels okay, try:

- Getting a table at a casual restaurant
- Going during busy lunch hours (you blend in more)
- Bringing a book or journal if it helps you feel

less exposed
- Practicing enjoying your food and the experience

I'm not going to lie - this one might feel weird the first few times. But I promise you, restaurant staff see solo diners all the time, and other customers aren't paying attention to you.

The "Treat Yourself" Solo Activity

Pick something you actually enjoy and do it alone:

Ideas:

- Go to a museum or art gallery.
- Browse a bookstore for as long as you want
- Get a massage or facial.
- Go to a matinee movie.
- Visit a farmers' market.
- Take yourself shopping (not stress shopping, fun shopping)
- Get your nails done

The key: Pick something you genuinely want to do, not something you think you "should" do alone.

Why this works:

- You're associating being alone with pleasure, not punish- ment.
- You get to go at your own pace.
- You might discover you enjoy things differently when alone.

- You're proving that you can have fun by yourself

Handling the Uncomfortable Moments

Because there will be some. Here's how to get through them:

If you feel anxious:

- Remind yourself this is temporary.
- Take slow, deep breaths.
- Look around and notice five specific things (the color of that person's shirt, the sound of the coffee machine, the smell of pastries)
- Remember that anxiety isn't dangerous, just uncomfortable

If you feel lonely:

- Please take a look at the difference between being alone and being lonely.
- Remind yourself that you chose to be here.
- Think about how you'll feel proud of yourself for doing this.
- Remember that you can connect with people later if you want

If you feel like people are staring:

- They're probably not, but even if they are, so what?
- You're not doing anything wrong or embarrassing.

- Some people might admire your confidence
- Their opinions don't determine your worth.

If you want to leave:

- That's okay! You don't have to force yourself to stay if you're truly uncomfortable.
- Even staying for 5 minutes is an accomplishment.
- You can always try again another day.
- There's no shame in building up slowly

The Magic of Choice

Here's something beautiful that happens when you start doing things alone: you realize how many choices you make automatically to accommodate other people.

When you're alone:

- You can linger as long as you want at the museum exhibit that fascinates you.
- You can order precisely what you're craving, not what's easy to share
- You can change your mind about where to go without needing to explain yourself.
- You can sit in comfortable silence without feeling like you need to make conversation.

This isn't about becoming antisocial. It's about remembering that you have preferences, desires, and a unique way of experiencing the world.

Building Your Solo Activit5 List

Make a list of things you should try doing alone. Start with things that feel manageable and add things that feel more challenging:

Manageable:

- Coffee shop sitting
- Solo walk in the park.
- Getting groceries during quiet hours
- Library browsing

Slightly Challenging:

- Lunch at a counter
- Movie matinee
- Museum visit
- Shopping for something fun

Feels Scary but Maybe Doable Eventually:

- Dinner at a restaurant
- Concert or live music
- Day trip somewhere
- Weekend activity you've always wanted to try

The Rule: You never have to do anything on this list. It's just brainstorming. However, having options can be helpful when you're feeling brave.

What Success Looks Like

Success is not:

- Feeling completely comfortable and confident

immediately

- Never feeling awkward or self-conscious
- Becoming someone who prefers to do everything alone

Success IS:

- Trying one small thing, even if it feels scary
- Lasting longer each time before you want to escape
- Starting to notice moments where you enjoy yourself
- Making decisions based on what you want, not just on avoiding being alone
- Building evidence that you can handle being by yourself in the world

The Unexpected Benefits

Here's what might surprise you about doing things alone:

- You notice more details when you're not focused on conversation.
- You move at your own pace, which can be a relaxing experience.
- You might discover new things about what you like and don't like
- Other people sometimes approach you more easily when you're alone (if you want that)
- You feel proud of yourself for being brave.
- You start to see being alone as freedom rather

than punishment

When Other People Comment

Occasionally, someone might say something about you being alone. Usually, it's innocent curiosity, but sometimes it can feel judgmental.

Common comments and responses:

- "Are you here by yourself?" → "Yes, I'm enjoying some solo time!"
- "Didn't anyone want to come with you?" → "I prefer doing this alone."
- "I could never eat alone, I'd be too embarrassed." → "It's peaceful once you try it."

Remember: You don't owe anyone an explanation for being alone. You're not doing anything wrong or strange.

Your Solo Adventure Plan

This week, pick ONE thing from this list to try:

- ☐ Sit in a coffee shop for 10 minutes without immediately using your phone
- ☐ Take a 15-minute solo walk somewhere pleasant
- ☐ Eat lunch at a counter (deli, café, diner)
- ☐ Browse a bookstore or library for 20 minutes
- ☐ Go to a museum or gallery during a quiet time
- ☐ Take yourself out for ice cream or a treat.

After you do it:

- Could you write down how it went?
- What felt hard?
- What surprised you?
- What would you do differently next time?
- What felt good about it?
- How do you feel about yourself for trying?

If it doesn't go perfectly: That's normal! The first time I ate alone at a restaurant, I was so nervous I could barely taste my food. But I did it, and each time after, it got a little easier.

Building Toward Book 2

These solo activities are building something significant: the knowledge that you can not only survive being alone, but enjoy it.

In Book 2 of this series ("You're Not Alone"), we'll go much deeper into transforming your entire relationship with solitude. But these small acts of courage you're doing now? They're the foundation that makes all that deeper work possible.

You're proving to yourself that being alone doesn't make you weird, pathetic, or doomed to loneliness. You're just a person who enjoys their own company sometimes, and there's absolutely nothing wrong with that.

There's something extraordinary about it.

Your Solo Adventure Planning

This Week, I'm Going to Try: (Pick just one!)

- ☐ Coffee shop sitting (10 minutes)
- ☐ Solo walk (15 minutes)
- ☐ Lunch counter meal
- ☐ Library/bookstore browse
- ☐ Museum/gallery visit
- ☐ Treat myself activity: _____

When: (Pick a specific day and time) Day: _____
Time:_____

How I'll Prepare:

- What will I wear that makes me feel confident?
- What time of day would work best for you?
- Do I need to scout the location first?
- What will I tell myself if I feel nervous?

My Backup Plan: If it feels too overwhelming:

- I can leave early, and that's okay.
- I can try again another day.
- I can start even smaller next time.
- I did something brave just by trying

After My Solo Adventure: What happened:

_____

_____

How I felt during:

_____

_____

What surprised me:

_____

_____

What I'm proud of:

_____

_____

What I might try next:

_____

_____

One thing I learned about myself:

_____

_____

Remember: There's no wrong way to do this. Every attempt is brave, whether it goes perfectly or not.

Chapter 6

Creating Your Support System (Because You Don't Have to Do This Alone)

Here's something that might seem backward: learning to be comfortable alone is easier when you have good people supporting you.

I know, I know. "Cheryl, I'm trying not to need people so much!" But here's the thing - there's a vast difference between desperately clinging to people to avoid being alone, and having healthy support while you build your independence.

Think of it like learning to swim. You don't just throw someone in the deep end and hope for the best. You have a supportive instructor, maybe some flotation devices, and people cheering you on from the sidelines. Once you can swim, you don't need all that support anymore - but having it while you learn makes the whole process possible.

The Difference Between Healthy and Unhealthy Support

Unhealthy dependence looks like:

- Needing someone available 24/7 to text or call
- Panicking when people don't respond immediately
- Making plans with anyone, even people you don't like, to avoid being alone
- Staying in bad relationships because being single = alone
- Getting angry with people for having their own lives and not always being available.

Healthy support looks like:

- Having a few trusted people who understand what you're working on
- Knowing you can reach out when you need it, without expecting immediate responses
- People who encourage your independence rather than enable your dependence
- Friends who celebrate your progress in learning to be alone
- A support system that's there when you need it, but doesn't make you feel weak for needing it

Who to Tell About This Work

You don't need to announce to everyone that you're "working on your fear of being alone." But having a few key people who understand can make a huge difference.

Good candidates:

- Close friends who are emotionally mature
- Family members who are supportive (not everyone has this, and that's okay)
- A therapist or counselor, if you have one
- People who've done their own personal growth work
- Anyone who's shown they can listen without immediately trying to "fix" you

What to tell them: "I'm working on getting more comfortable spending time by myself. It's something I've always struggled with, and I'm trying to build up my confidence gradually. Sometimes I might need encouragement, and sometimes I might want to share how it's going."

What NOT to tell them: You don't need to go into all the details of your fear, your childhood, or how bad it's been. Please keep it simple and focus on what you're working toward, rather than dwelling on everything wrong.

The Check-In System

Having someone check in on your progress can be incredibly motivating.

How it works:

- Pick one person who's good at being supportive without being pushy.
- Tell them about your small goals ("I'm going to try sitting in a coffee shop alone this week")
- Ask if they can check in afterward to see how it went.
- Make it clear that you want encouragement, not advice (unless you ask for it)

Sample text exchange: You: "Trying my first solo coffee shop visit today. Nervous but excited!" Friend: "You've got this! Can't wait to hear how it goes." (Later) You: "I did it! Felt weird at first but nice by the end." Friend: "I'm so proud of you! That's huge!"

Dealing with People Who Don't Get It

Unfortunately, not everyone will understand why you need to work on being alone. You might get responses like:

- "Just get a boyfriend/girlfriend, problem solved!"
- "I don't get why you want to be alone; that sounds depress- ing."
- "You're overthinking this, just stop worrying about it."

How to handle this:

- Remember that their response is about their

relationship with solitude, not yours.

- You don't have to explain or defend your growth work.
- It's okay to say, "It's something I'm working on," and change the subject.
- Focus your energy on the people who do support you

Online Communities (*Yes, Really*)

I know, I know. "Get off the internet and learn to be alone!" However, online communities can be beneficial for this work.

Where to look:

- Reddit communities about personal growth, anxiety, or self-improvement
- Facebook groups for people working on independence
- Apps like Meetup for people with similar goals
- Forums for introverts or people doing personal develop- ment work

What these communities offer:

- Proof that you're not the only person dealing with this
- Ideas for solo activities to try
- Encouragement from people who understand
- A place to celebrate small wins with people who get why they matter

The balance: Use these communities for support and inspiration, but don't use them to avoid the actual work of being alone. They're a tool, not a substitute for real-life practice.

Professional Support (When to Consider It)

If your fear of being alone is intense, or if you're dealing with other anxiety or depression issues, talking to a professional can be incredibly helpful.

Consider therapy if:

- Your fear of being alone is impacting major life decisions.
- You're having panic attacks when alone.
- You're staying in harmful relationships to avoid being single.
- You have thoughts of self-harm when you're alone.
- Your anxiety about being alone is getting worse instead of better.
- You suspect trauma or deeper issues are involved

What therapy can offer:

- Professional tools for managing anxiety
- Help processing past experiences that contribute to the fear.
- A safe space to explore deeper issues
- Medications are needed if anxiety is severe.

- Specialized techniques like EMDR or CBT

Finding a therapist:

- Ask friends for recommendations.
- Use online directories like Psychology Today.
- Contact your insurance company to find out which providers are covered.
- Look for therapists who specialize in anxiety or attachment issues.
- Don't be afraid to "shop around" until you find someone you click with

Building Independence Within Relationships

If you're in a romantic relationship, learning to be alone can make your relationship stronger, but your partner might not understand that at first.

What partners might worry about:

- "Does this mean she doesn't want to spend time with me?"
- "Is she planning to leave me?"
- "Am I not enough for her?"

How to reassure them:

- Explain that this is about being a healthier, more complete person, not about pulling away from them.
- Let them know that your goal is to choose to be with them from a place of want, not desperate

need.

- Include them in your progress - tell them about your solo adventures and what you're learning.
- Make sure you're still making time for connection and intimacy

Setting healthy boundaries:

- It's okay to spend some evenings alone, even if you live together.
- You can have solo hobbies and interests.
- You don't need to include your partner in every single activity.
- Healthy relationships include togetherness AND individual growth

The Friend Who Always Wants to "Help"

You know this person - the one who can't stand to see you alone and constantly tries to rescue you from solitude.

They say things like:

- "You shouldn't be alone, come over!"
- "I'll keep you company so you don't have to be by yourself."
- "Being alone isn't healthy; humans need other people."

How to handle this:

- Appreciate their good intentions while

protecting your growth.

- "I appreciate that you care about me. Right now, I'm working on getting comfortable with alone time, so I'm going to stay in tonight."
- Be consistent - if you keep accepting their "rescue" offers, they won't learn that you're serious about this.
- If they can't respect your boundaries, you might need to limit contact while you're doing this work.

Creating New Types of Social Plans

As you become more comfortable being alone, you may find that your social needs shift. You might want:

Quality over quantity:

- Fewer social plans, but more meaningful ones
- Time with people who energize you rather than drain you
- Social activities that align with your interests and values

Balance:

- Some solo time and some social time, rather than constant togetherness
- Permission to leave social events when you're ready, not when others are
- Social plans that feel like a choice rather than a necessity

Honesty:

- Being able to say "I'm looking forward to a quiet night in"
- Declining invitations without elaborate excuses
- Suggesting activities that you want to do

Your Support System Action Plan

Identify Your Support People: List 2-3 people who could be supportive of this work:

1._____

2._____

What You'll Tell Them: Write a simple script for explaining what you're working on:

Your Check-In Person: Who can you ask to check in on your progress?

Name: _____ How often:_____

Boundaries You Need: What do you need to ask for from friends/family?

- More understanding when you choose solo time
- Fewer "rescue" attempts when you're alone
- Encouragement rather than advice
- Other: _____

Professional Support: Would you benefit from talking to a counselor about this?

☐ Yes, I'd like to explore this option

☐ Maybe, if things don't improve with these self-help strategies

☐ No, I feel like I can handle this on my own right now

The Beautiful Irony

Here's what I've found to be true: the more comfortable you become with being alone, the better your relationships get.

When you're not desperately avoiding solitude, you:

- You can approach relationships as a choice, not a necessity.
- You're more present with people because you're not anxiously clinging to them.
- Can appreciate others without trying to use them to avoid yourself
- Become someone others enjoy being around because you're not needy or desperate.

You don't lose your connections when you learn to be alone. You gain the freedom to choose them from a place of love rather than fear. And that makes all the difference.

Your Support System Worksheet

My Support Team:

Person 1: _____

Relationship to me: _____

Why they'd be good support: _____

What I need from them: _____

Person 2: _____

Relationship to me: _____

Why they'd be good support: _____

What I need from them:_____

Person 3: _____

Relationship to me: _____

Why they'd be good support: _____

What I need from them:_____

My Script: "I'm working on getting more comfortable spend- ing time by myself. It's something I've always found challenging, and I'm taking small steps to build my confidence. I'd appreciate your encouragement as I work on this."

Boundaries I Need to Set:

With friends: _____

With family: _____

With romantic partner: _____

With myself: _____

Professional Support Consideration:

☐   I want to find a therapist to help with this

☐   I'm not ready for therapy, but I might consider

it later

☐ I have a therapist and will discuss this with them

☐ I don't think I need professional help right now

Red Flags to Watch For:

If any of these happen, I'll consider getting professional help:

- Panic attacks when alone
- Thoughts of self-harm
- Unable to make any progress after trying these techniques
- Fear is getting worse instead of better
- Impacting major life decisions (jobs, relationships, living situation)

Remember: Asking for support isn't a sign of weakness - it's a sign of wisdom.

Let's wrap this up with your next steps...

Conclusion

Look How Far You've Come (And Where You're Headed)

Hey there, beautiful soul.

Take a moment and think back to when you first picked up this book. Remember that feeling? The mixture of hope and fear, the wondering if you were broken somehow, the exhaustion from constantly avoiding being alone with yourself?

Now look at where you are. You've:

1. Name what you're dealing with instead of just suffering in silence
2. Understood where your fear came from (and that it's not your fault)
3. Started practicing tiny moments of solitude
4. Built a foundation for feeling safe when you're alone
5. Maybe even tried doing something by yourself out in the world
6. Created or identified support for this journey

That's not nothing. That's everything.

You're Not the Same Person Who Started This Book

I know it might not feel like a dramatic transformation and that's okay. Real change rarely announces itself with fireworks and sudden revelations. Instead, it shows up in small moments:

- The split second of peace you felt during your five-minute sit practice.
- The time you chose to stay home instead of scrambling to make plans
- The moment you realized you were okay in the coffee shop by yourself.
- The day you didn't immediately reach for your phone when you were alone.
- The first time being alone felt more like freedom than punishment

These tiny shifts? They're the seeds of profound change.

What You've Proven to Yourself

Through doing this work, you've gathered evidence that con- tradicts your old fears:

Old belief: "I can't handle being alone."

New evidence: "I can sit with myself for increasingly longer periods"

Old belief: "Being alone means something's wrong with me."

New evidence: "Lots of healthy, wonderful people value alone time"

Old belief: "I'll fall apart if I'm by myself."

New evidence: "I've felt difficult emotions while alone and survived them."

Old belief: "People will judge me for being alone."

New evidence: "Most people don't notice or care, and some admire it."

Old belief: "I need other people to feel okay."

New evidence: "I can create my sense of peace and comfort"

The Skills You've Built

You might not realize it, but you've developed some pretty impressive capabilities:

Emotional regulation: You can sit with uncomfortable feelings without immediately trying to escape them

Self-awareness: You can recognize when your fear is showing up and what triggers it

Self-compassion: You've learned to be kind to yourself through difficult moments instead of beating yourself up

Courage: You've done things that scared you, which is the definition of bravery

Mindfulness: You can be present with your experience instead of constantly distracting yourself

Independence: You've started making choices based on what you want, not just on avoiding being alone

These aren't small accomplishments. These are life skills that will serve you for a lifetime.

This is Just the Beginning

Here's something I want you to understand: what you've done in this book is build the foundation. You've laid the groundwork for a completely different relationship with solitude.

But there's so much more available to you.

In Book 2 of this series ("You're Not Alone: Overcoming Monophobia and Embracing the Gift of Solitude"), we go deeper into everything:

- Comprehensive transformation tools that will help you not just tolerate solitude, but genuinely enjoy it
- Deep healing work for the underlying wounds that created this fear
- Advanced practices for turning alone time into your most significant source of strength and creativity
- Complete relationship makeover - learning to connect with others from wholeness instead of neediness
- Workbook exercises that guide you through profound internal shifts
- The spiritual dimensions of solitude and how

they can transform your entire life

Think of this book as learning to dog-paddle, and Book 2 as becoming a confident swimmer who loves being in the water. But here's the thing: you couldn't have done that deeper work without this foundation. You needed to prove to yourself first that you could handle being alone at all. Now that you have that evidence, you're ready for the transformation work that will change everything.

Your Next Steps (Choose Your Adventure)

You have a few options for how to move forward:

Option 1: Keep Practicing What You've Learned

1. Continue your daily alone time practice.
2. Keep trying new solo activities.
3. Deepen your comfort with the skills you've built.
4. You can use this book as a reference when you need some help.
5. Move to Book 2 when you feel ready for deeper work

Option 2: Jump into Book 2 Now

1. If you're feeling motivated and ready for comprehensive change
2. If you want more tools and deeper healing practices
3. If you're excited about transforming your entire relation- ship with solitude

4. The foundation you've built here will make everything in Book 2 more effective.

Option 3: Get Additional Support

- Work with a therapist who understands anxiety and attach- ment issues.
- Join a support group or online community.
- You can use the companion workbook for more structured practice.
- Combine professional help with continued self-help work

There's no wrong choice here. Trust yourself to know what feels right.

What I Want You to Remember

As you continue this journey, please remember:

1. **You're not broken.** You never were. You're a sensitive and thoughtful person who has developed understandable coping strategies for a very human fear.
2. **Your pace is perfect.** Some people will progress through this work more quickly, while others will do so more slowly. Your timeline is precisely right for you.
3. **Setbacks are normal.** There will be days when the old fear feels just as strong as ever. That doesn't mean you're failing - it means you're human.
4. **You deserve solitude that feels peaceful.** Not

just toler- able, not just manageable, but nourishing and restorative.

5. **You deserve relationships that feel free—**connections based on love and choice, not fear and desperation.

6. **You deserve a life that feels authentically yours—o**ne where your decisions stem from your values and desires, not from a fear of being alone.

A Letter to Your Future Self

I want you to imagine yourself a year from now. You've contin- ued this work, perhaps with Book 2, perhaps with professional support, or perhaps just by maintaining the practices you've learned.

That future version of you:

- Makes plans based on what they want to do
- Enjoys evenings at home without feeling like they're miss- ing out
- They choose relationships that enrich their lives rather than fill a desperate void.
- Feels curious about their thoughts and feelings instead of being afraid of them
- They have discovered interests and aspects of themselves they never knew existed.
- Radiates a quiet confidence that comes from knowing they can handle whatever comes up

That person isn't some fantasy version of you. That's

who you're becoming right now, with every small act of courage, every moment you choose to sit with yourself instead of running away, every time you treat yourself with kindness instead of judgment.

From Me to You

I'm so proud of you for doing this work. I know how scary it felt at the beginning. I know how many times you might have wanted to quit. I know how vulnerable it is to examine the parts of yourself that feel broken or shameful.

But you did it anyway. You showed up for yourself in the most fundamental way possible by learning to be present with who you are.

That takes incredible courage, and I want you to acknowledge yourself for that.

The Invitation

As you close this book and think about what comes next, I want to leave you with this thought:

Your fear of being alone has been trying to protect you, but it's also been keeping you small. It's been preventing you from discovering the incredible person you are when no one else is around. It's been stopping you from making choices that align with your authentic desires. It's been limiting your capacity for deep, genuine connections with others.

But all of that is changing now. Every time you choose to sit with yourself instead of immediately seeking distraction, you're choosing growth over comfort.

Every time you do something alone that used to scare you, you're choosing courage over fear. Every time you treat yourself with compassion instead of criticism, you're choosing love over judgment. These choices are transforming you, one small moment at a time.

The invitation now is to keep going. To keep choosing yourself. To keep believing that you're worth the effort it takes to heal this old wound. Because you are, you are so worth it.

What's Waiting for You

On the other side of this fear is a version of yourself that you can barely imagine right now:

- Someone who genuinely enjoys their own company. Some- one who makes decisions from a place of inner knowing rather than external pressure. Someone who can be truly present with others because they're not desperately trying to avoid themselves.
- Someone who has discovered that the very thing they feared most - being alone - is actually where they found their greatest strength, creativity, and peace.
- That person is not far away. You're already becoming them. Keep going, beautiful. The best parts of this journey are yet to come.

With so much love and faith in you, Cheryl

Your Graduation Ceremony (Yes, Really)

Before you move on from this book, I want you to acknowledge what you've accomplished. This isn't silly - it's necessary. You've done brave, challenging work that deserves recognition.

Complete these statements:

When I started this book, I felt:

_____

_____

The thing I've learned about myself is:

_____

_____

The hardest part of this work has been:

_____

_____

Something I can do now that I couldn't do before:

_____

_____

What I'm most proud of myself for:

_____

_____

How I want to continue growing:

_____

_____

Your Commitment to Yourself:

I commit to continuing this work by:

- ☐ Practicing the skills I've learned regularly
- ☐ Reading Book 2 in this series
- ☐ Seeking professional support
- ☐ Being patient and kind with myself as I keep growing
- ☐ Celebrating small wins along the way
- ☐ Other: _____

Your Reminder for Hard Days:

Write yourself a note to read when the old fears feel strong: Dear Me,

You've already proven that you can handle being alone. Remember when ? You did that. You can handle whatever comes up. You're braver than you think, stronger than you feel, and more loved than you know - especially by yourself.

Keep going. You've got this. Love, Me

Date: _____

Afterword

Preview: What Awaits You in Book 2

"Facing the Fear of Being Alone: How to Turn Solitude into Strength"

Ready to take this work to the next level? Book 2 offers:

Deep Transformation Work

- Comprehensive healing exercises that address the root causes of your fear
- Advanced mindfulness and self-compassion practices
- Tools for rewiring your nervous system's response to solitude

Practical Mastery

- A complete workbook section with 50+ exercises
- 30-day transformation challenges
- Step-by-step guides for turning solitude into your super- power

Relationship Revolution

- How to transform all your relationships when you're no longer needy
- Dating and partnership from a place of wholeness
- Setting healthy boundaries without guilt

Creative and Spiritual Awakening

- Using solitude for a creative breakthrough
- The spiritual dimensions of alone time
- Discovering who you are beneath all the noise

Real-Life Integration

- Advanced solo activities and adventures
- Building a life that honors both connection and solitude
- Becoming someone others admire for your independence and peace

Community and Support

- Access to online resources and community
- Additional tools for different learning styles
- Ongoing support for your transformation journey

Book 2 picks up exactly where this book leaves off. You've built the foundation - now it's time to construct the beautiful life that's possible when you're no longer afraid of your own company.

Resources for Your Journey

Emergency Support

If you ever feel overwhelmed or unsafe:

- Crisis Text Line: Text HOME to 741741
- National Suicide Prevention Lifeline: 988
- Your local emergency services: 911

Professional Support

- Psychology Today Therapist Directory: psychologyto- day.com
- Anxiety and Depression Association: adaa.org
- Your healthcare provider for referrals

Recommended Reading

- "Self-Compassion" by Kristin Neff
- "The Gifts of Imperfection" by Brené Brown
- "Radical Acceptance" by Tara Brach

Connect with the Author

- Website: cheryltlong. site
- Blog: deardaughterslovesmom.com
- Newsletter signup for bonus content and encouragement

What's Next in the Series

- **Book 2:** "Facing the Fear of Being Alone: How to Turn Solitude into Strength"

- **Book 3:** "Embracing Your Authentic Self: From People- Pleasing to Personal Power" (coming soon)
- **Book 4:** "Healing Your Relationship with Love: From Codependency to Conscious Connection" (coming soon)

One Final Thought

Thank you for trusting me to walk alongside you on this part of your journey. Thank you for having the courage to face what scared you most. Thank you for believing that change was possible, even when it felt impossible.

Your willingness to heal doesn't just transform your own life

- it gives everyone around you permission to heal too. Your courage creates ripples you'll never even know about.

Keep going, beautiful soul. Your most authentic, peaceful, creative, and connected life is waiting for you on the other side of this fear.

And you're already so much closer than you think.

With infinite love and belief in you, Cheryl

About the Author

Cheryl T. Long isn't a licensed therapist or psychology expert— she's something even better for this work: someone who has lived exactly what you're experiencing.

For most of her adult life, Cheryl moved from one relation- ship directly into the next, terrified of being truly alone. As a mother, she filled her house with her children's friends and constant activity, not just because she loved having kids around, but because the silence felt unbearable.

It wasn't until her third marriage ended and her husband passed away that Cheryl was forced, for the first time, to depend entirely on herself. What began as her greatest fear became her most profound transformation—learning not just to tolerate her own company, but to enjoy it genuinely.

Now Cheryl writes with the warmth of your wisest friend and the authority of someone who has walked the exact path her readers are on. She lives in Philadelphia with her family, where she continues to value both solitude and connection as essential components of a fulfilling life.

Connect with Cheryl at **cheryltlong. site** and **deardaughters lovesmom.com**

www.ingramcontent.com/pod-product-compliance
Lightning Source LLC
Chambersburg PA
CBHW060343050426
42449CB00011B/2816